MASTER THE ART OF PUBLIC SPEAKING

1. How to Read and Use this Book

A basic and successful methodology for getting sorted out your discourse goes like this:

1. Intro: Tell them what you will tell them.
2. Body: Tell them.
3. Conclusion: Tell them what you told them.

In due style, I will start this book by first letting you know what I'm going to tell you.

Each section of the book will be organized similarly:

First – we breakdown down the particular space of correspondence we will address. This incorporates characterizing the ideas, pinpointing the issue, and recognizing the best answer for work towards.

Second– we will examine the procedures, the structures, and ways of coming to the ideal solution.

Third – we will forever close with a thing to do on how you can practice.

You can peruse every part, stop, and afterward practice. Or then again, you can peruse the book as far as possible and pick the regions that are explicit to your necessities and practice those regions. The speed at which you go will be totally dependent upon you. Notwithstanding, you genuinely should rehearse. Assuming that you don't rehearse, you can't anticipate improving. Understanding the ideas is the initial phase in further developing your abilities, however to genuinely improve yourself will require practice, very much like in actual exercise or obtaining some other skills.

In certain practices, it will be unbelievably useful to have an associate or companion assist you with trip. Having someone else's perspective can assist with spotting things that you might be disregarding. Obviously, it would be more useful in the event that your companion comprehended the ideas and what you are attempting to accomplish in talking. All things considered, I would suggest that you share this book with the person in question, or you can show your companion what you are realizing. Assuming you can show another person, that makes your abilities more grounded. Approach using this book with the outlook that you will show this data to your companion. The best trial of understanding an idea is attempting to instruct it to somebody else.

This ought to be direct and simple to do: read this book and practice. Assuming you can do that, you ought to accomplish a quantifiable improvement in your correspondence capacities! Presently, before you say a word, we should initially comprehend YOU.

2. What are your goals?
"It's the chance of having a little glimpse of heaven that makes life interesting."
– Paulo Coelho, The Alchemist

Why are you understanding this? What are your objectives? To take advantage of this book, contemplate your objectives at the present time. Have a go at expressing both wide objectives and explicit goals.

List them out (it tends to be more than 3):

1.
2.
3.

Don't skirt this activity. This is significant so you have the best experience utilizing this book and improving your skills.
Here is a rundown of objectives from my students:

.

Move up the ladder and progress in my career

.

Be charismatic, poised, and confident

.

Improve my presentation, speaking, and writing

.

Win this competition

.

Organize my content and the thoughts in my head

.

Speak articulately and passionately

.

Have better conversations with my colleagues

.

Be more coherent when speaking

.

Know how to frame and organize content

.

Demonstrate leadership

.

Write strong and effective emails

.

Use colorful language like common idioms and expressions

.

Answer interview questions well

.

Have great responses when managers throw out questions

.

Not make mistakes in communicating

.Want to be able to communicate well when opportunities present themselves

If your mind started to wonder at all the different possibilities, then you are thinking correctly. We will address this eventually, however as you contemplate your objectives, understand that further developing your relational abilities will apply to different aspects of your life. For instance, assuming you objective is to introduce better to your associates during work gatherings, having that further developed ability will give you trust in talking in ordinary circumstances outside of work. As we've examined, correspondence is a crucial human component that isn't just present in the working environment. It is something that we use by and large each and every day. Having these objectives and endeavoring to accomplish them will fan out the advantages into different parts of your life. Later you've contemplated your objectives, we would now be able to move on.

3. Be Honest About Your Weaknesses

"We should initially find and talk about the shortcoming, and afterward we should proceed to reconstruct everything."
– Arnold Schwarzenegger, 7x Mr. Olympia Champion

Good. Since you have pondered your objectives, you ought to have an unmistakable vision and inspiration on why you are perusing and you ought to guess why you will make a move. Above all, how about we stop to assess a few limits. Presently comes the part where you must be straightforward with yourself.

You are perusing this book on purpose: you need to further develop your abilities. We will distinguish qualities next, yet chipping away at the shortcomings first offers us the chance to accomplish high measures of upgrades. How about we evaluate: What are your concerns with regards to public talking? In what spaces of your correspondence would you say you are awkward with? Characterizing these obstructions will give us incredible progress into making improvements.

Ray Dalio, the tycoon mutual funds chief has extraordinary insight with regards to resolving individual issues: He says, "Recognizing issues resembles observing diamonds inserted in puzzles; assuming you address the riddles, you will get the jewels that will make your life much better." This might be somewhat difficult, however we should rip the Band-Aid off quick and with genuineness. What are the issues that you face with regards to communicating?
 Here are a few inquiries to pose to yourself while recognizing your spaces of improvement:

.

What parts of public speaking makes you

.

uncomfortable? Where do you feel weak in public speaking?

.

Which areas are you not confident

.

about? Where do you hesitate?

.

How well do people understand you when you are speaking?

As you did with your objectives, rattle off somewhere around 3 spaces of enhancements to concentrate on:

1.
2.
3.

Here are some of the common problems that my students state: .

Lags in self-marketing

.

Struggles to be articulate Weakness

.

in presenting to people

.

Challenges with spontaneous talking

.

Hesitation to ask questions spontaneously

- Fear or nervousness when speaking

- Email messages are not written clearly enough

- Preparing presentations

- Using visuals in presentations

- Impromptu speaking, answering questions

- Articulating to the audience

- Remaining too quiet during meetings

- Fear of asking bad questions

Limited facial expressions, need to smile more

Not enough vocal variety

Confidence in giving personal pitch and story

Overall fluency

Talking too fast

Using too many filler words ("um's/uh's")

4. **Build on Your Strengths**

Improving your abilities in anything is an iterative interaction. You ought to alternate between the parts and ideas of this book, as you find new things about yourself. Since you have finished the activity in recognizing your shortcomings, how about we distinguish and expand on your qualities. Everybody is great at something. At the point when you talk and impart, it is an incredible chance to feature your strengths. Communicating is the second where you are allowed to put yourself out there. Indeed, you might have shortcomings, however you additionally have qualities. If you combine your strengths and weaknesses, and you express yourself freely, then people begin to see your personality.

Similarly we recognized your objectives and shortcomings, we should do likewise for your strengths.
Ask yourself questions such as:

.

What are you good at?

.

What can you talk endlessly about?

.

What makes you smile when you talk?

.

What questions do your friends or colleagues ask you about?

List out no less than 3 of your

qualities: 1.
2.
3.

Here are some strengths that my students have listed: .

Strong technical knowledge

.

Being a team player

.

Experience with various companies

.

Many years of experience in the industry

.

Very analytical

.

Passionate about work

.

Worked with international teams

.

Very good problem-solver

- Taking initiative

- Leadership

- Technology acumen

- Working with different types and levels of people

- Proven impact for team

- Confidence in skills

- Real experience

- Can hire people

- Can program in many languages

- Software development

- Led big projects

- Need minimal supervision

- Work independently

Congratulations, you are presently headed to turning into a more compelling communicator. The initial step is to be acutely mindful of your present real factors. What are you great at, terrible at, and where would you like to wind up? As such, what are your qualities, shortcomings, and objectives? The place of these activities is to take a gander at yourself impartially, the same way I would on the off chance that I were showing you one-on-one. Since you are involving this book as an aide, you will be your own mentor. A mentor takes a gander at your exhibition according to a third individual's perspective and guides you en route. You are currently your own mentor. For that reason you must be straightforward and evaluate yourself before we get into different ideas of communication.

If you need, set aside some additional effort to ensure you have these basics down. Truly comprehend the regions that you are slacking in, so you know which regions to improve. Be positive about your qualities, with the goal that you know how to best feature yourself. What's more, be clear concerning the objectives of why you are doing this, so you stay spurred to improve your abilities.

Now that you comprehend yourself better, how about we start with the brilliant individual pitch.

5. The Golden Personal Pitch

The principal discourse I request that every one of my understudies present is the individual pitch. Recollect that TED stage in the start of the book. Place yourself on that stage. Remember, that stage is dependent on your situation: it might be your work conference room, at a Starbucks as you pitch your services to a potential customer, in a job interview, out to lunch with your friends, or you may actually be speaking in front of three thousand people on a massive stage fit for symphonies. Here is your freedom to exhibit yourself. What do you say? Where do you begin?

Experience from working with my understudies lets me know that you presumably have an overall comprehension of what you will say, however when you say it, you will more often than not continue to talk and it seems as though you're out of control. You may be saying filler words like "um" or "uh" without staying alert. You additionally have the right substance
– for instance, solid work experience
– yet you don't have the right design to explain yourself. So how would we improve? Structure.

Your story is exceptional. You have your very own accounts and encounters that make you exceptional. Structure is a system you can apply across various discourses. Utilize this design from the beginning. Then, if you want to add in your own style and flavor, feel free to make edits along the way. A significant part of correspondence to note is that correspondence is extremely close to home. It is you trading data with another person. What might be successful correspondence for your companion may not be the most ideal same for you. As you attempt and practice, you will ultimately find what accommodates your style best. This construction is an apparatus for you to impart your musings. Like developing a house, structure is the plan that puts the entirety of your words and thoughts together to construct an excellent mansion.

Your discourse ought to be separated into three fundamental sections:

1. Opening
2. Body
3. Conclusion

Each segment serves a particular purpose:
1. Opening- Tell them what you will tell them.
2. Body- Tell them.
3. Conclusion- Tell them what you told them.

Now, going into more profundity about each segment, the design of the show should look like this:

1. Opening
a. Captures crowd attention
b. Leads into discourse topic

2. Body
a. Main point
i. Subpoint
ii. Support material
b. Main point
i. Subpoint
ii. Support material
c. Main point
i. Subpoint

ii. Support material
3. Conclusion
a. Review or summary
b. Call to activity or vital statement

The place of this framework is to show you the best way to set up your discourse, to follow a sensible succession that your crowd can undoubtedly comprehend. Recollect that you can apply this structure for any show that you give. For the setting of this individual pitch, your target of the discourse is clear: *educate the crowd concerning yourself.* We should dive into much more insight regarding the particular pieces.

The Opening:
Studies have shown that individuals make decisions on whether they like a individual inside the initial seven seconds of meeting. Not to come down on you, but rather the initial feeling you give is exceptionally significant on you as a moderator. The opening ought to quickly draw in the crowd. Recall any show that you have endured. For what reason do you recollect it, what do you recall about it? Chances are, that moderator effectively caught your consideration and presently you actually recollect it.

Good instances of openings can be:

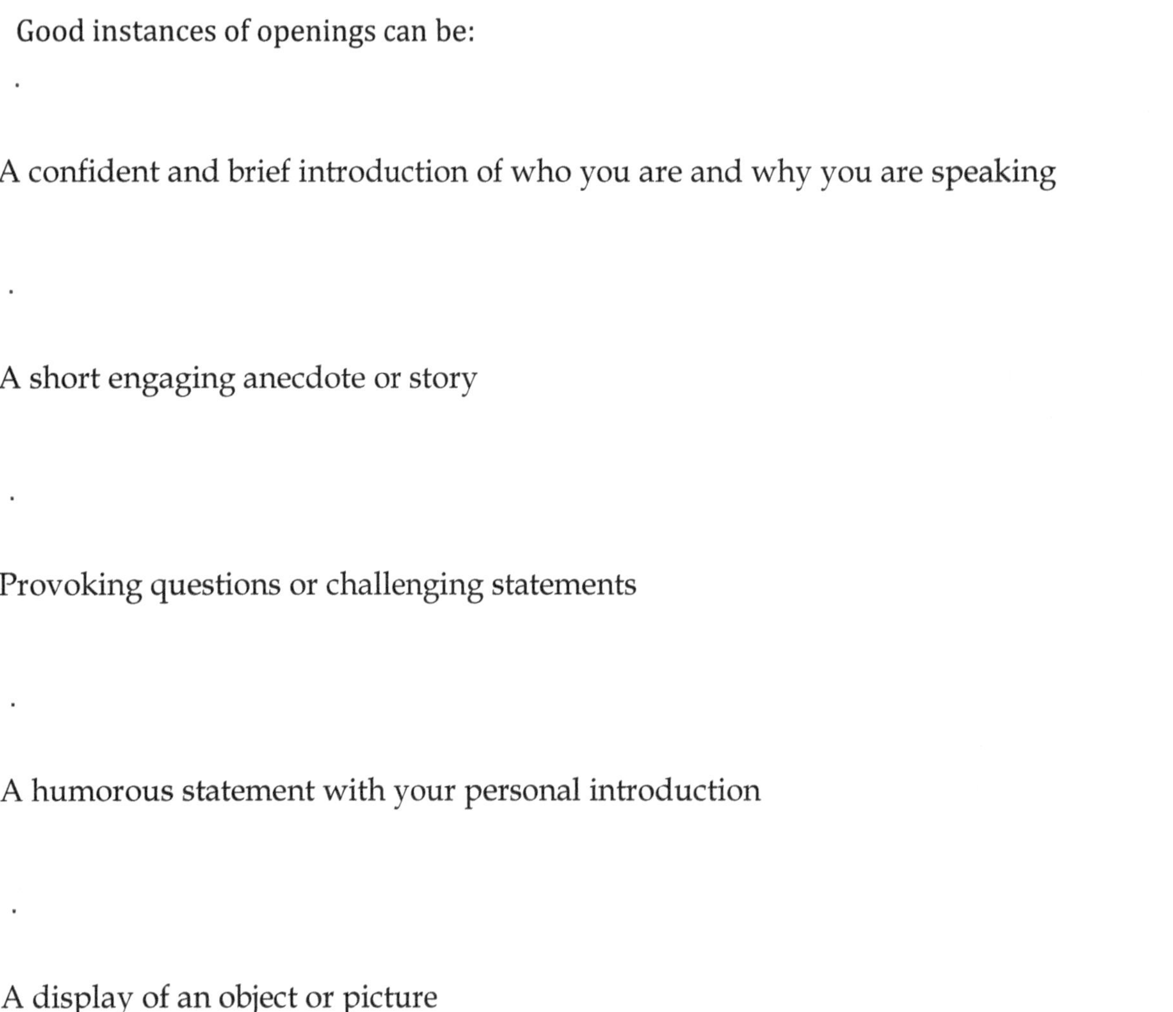

.

A confident and brief introduction of who you are and why you are speaking

.

A short engaging anecdote or story

.

Provoking questions or challenging statements

.

A humorous statement with your personal introduction

.

A display of an object or picture

Any attention-grabbing materials that are related to your subject

Capturing the crowd's consideration implies that you connect with them in the thing you are saying. Do things that can make them giggle, grin, think, lift their hands. Identify with them promptly or interest their curiosity.

The Body
 This is the principle part of your discourse– this is the place where all the meat and juice are. The substance you place inside the body will fluctuate contingent upon how much time you have and what you are introducing. Normally, it is ideal to remain inside three to five central matters on the grounds that the human psyche typically recollects simply three to five fundamental realities during a speech.

You might have a great deal of data you need to introduce, however you should pick your best three to five. For this activity, we should accept we are involving three central matters in the body. Conceptualize and record every one of the focuses you need to introduce about yourself. This can likewise be taken from the qualities list that we distinguished before. Then, select the three most important points that you want to speak about.

The Subpoint
 Like a craftsman, you are attempting to illustrate yourself. The subpoint all the more plainly represents the thought or truth that it upholds. It gives clearness and accentuation to the central matter. This is the place where you can draw on explicit models and be more illustrative in your explanation.

 A decent method for contemplating it is that subpoints answer questions such as:

What do you mean?

Can you give me an example?

.

How did that happen?

Subpoints deliver the discourse really fascinating and assist the crowd with recalling the fundamental ideas.

The Support Material Support material follows each subpoint. This data helps support your case and can add mental representations to your speech.

Examples of supporting material include:

.

Numbers – Use statistics, percentages, or other types of numbers. It is easier to understand and remember that you "increased revenue by 75%" than if you said you "increased revenue by a lot."

.

Quotes – Use real life examples from what experts or your customers have said. If you are justifying why you have decided to make a change to your product, you can quote that 20 of your customers said they would spend more money if the product were like this. Or if there is an industry expert, you can quote her to support the point.

.

Examples – Everyone loves a good story. You can use a personal example, someone else's experiences, or other types of examples that support your point.

.

Visuals – Graphs, charts, and pictures can help the audience visualize what you are saying and add emphasis to your point. We'll talk more in depth about visuals in a later chapter.

.

Facts – Facts can be data points that are hard to argue with. For example, if you are saying that the majority of your customers would like it if your store were blue – and you supported the claim with the fact that 80% of all your customers have said that in a survey – then you have just made a compelling point.

The Conclusion:

The end is the place where you effectively express your idea. You need to remind your crowd what you went through today in your show – with the objective that they will recall every one of the significant focuses you've made. Try not to remember new data for the end, since you won't have the chance to support it. Every one of your focuses ought to have been made in the body, subpoints, and support material. The end is the point at which you "let them know what you told them" to support your message. You end ought to epitomize all of the data you've quite recently introduced for your memorable crowd. Your objective here is that when you say your final word, your crowd will think: "Goodness, that was great." Finish with confidence.
The design is finished with list items deliberately, on the grounds that you would rather not work out your discourse. This design is the way you begin fabricating your show. It is the skeleton to your speech.

An efficient discourse makes you:

.

Credible – Speakers who take time to prepare, organize, and practice their speeches are seen as more knowledgeable and believable.

.

Coherent – A poorly organized speech will likely cause you to ramble and be disjointed in your thoughts and ideas. Being organized allows you to present coherently.

Memorable – The audience can better identify and remember the points you have made.

Understandable – The audience knows exactly which points you are making and can follow along in their understanding of your speech.

Enjoyable – Like a good movie, audiences enjoy a presentation that nicely drives them from starting to end.

Here is an illustration of the Golden Personal Pitch layout from one of my students:
1. Opening– generally point: can oversee group to create a fruitful product
a. Years of involvement with major companies b. Leadership, innovation, group player
2. Body
a. Leadership– drove and oversaw different designing groups to fabricate items without any preparation in brief time of time

i. Led group in both US and China to assemble the organization's huge information platform

ii. Numbers: utilized information to decide and expanded our change rates by 3% b. Technology– information in inheritance and current technologies
i. Worked with different advancements: C, C++,

DCOM, Hadoop, Hive
ii. Example: made a model and progressed the
organization over to new technology c. Team player – extremely viable in working in
teams i. Worked with business and designing groups
to assemble an item from scratch ii. Example: accumulated client prerequisite
information to work with group to assemble
product
3. Conclusion
a. Leadership, innovation, group player
b. Can oversee group to foster an effective item

How To Practice:

Use this diagram and build it to accommodate your own pitch. Fill in the different places.
Be brief; the point isn't to work out your discourse. The point is to make a construction
for you to envision and work with.

Here is your clean canvas:

1. Opening
a. Captures crowd attention
b. Leads into discourse topic
2. Body

a. Main point
i. Subpoint
ii. Support material
b. Main point
i. Subpoint
ii. Support material
c. Main point
i. Subpoint
ii. Support material

3. Conclusion
a. Review or summary
b. Call to activity or vital statement

Extra Challenge:

Expand past your own pitch. Select a subject and make a discourse diagram utilizing a similar system. Pick something that you are intrigued in. Perhaps it's a warmed conversation you had with your companion concerning why fighters are superior to briefs, why your children ought to invest more energy doing schoolwork, why you fit the bill for this specific work, or any point that you are keen on. Practice this multiple times until you start to arrange focuses in your mind naturally at whatever point you ponder a theme. This is incredible preparing that can set you up in other areas.

Where else you can apply this:

·

Giving a presentation

·

Having a debate

·

Answering interview questions

·

Impromptu speaking

·

Thinking on your feet

Having a structure to work with gives your mind the ability to have a programmed perspective with regards to something. You would then be able to change and adjust your substance to whichever circumstance you are in.

6. Dissecting Greatness: Steve Jobs
"Assimilate what is valuable, dispose of what isn't, add what is particularly your own."
– Bruce Lee, Actor and Martial Artist

Now that you have gotten an opportunity to chip away at your own pitch, we can investigate genuine instances of what extraordinary discourses resemble. At the point when you consider renowned discourses heard all over the planet, there might be some that quickly rung a bell, like Martin Luther King Jr's."I Have A Dream" discourse. One more renowned speaker and visionary rings a bell — Steve Jobs.

Steve Jobs conveyed a strong initiation discourse to the alumni of Stanford University in 2005. Assuming you have not seen the speech, please go watch it online before continuing. If you have, it very well may be important to watch it once more (search"Steve Jobs Stanford
 Commencement Speech 2005").

The main thing you might see about his discourse is that he is perusing off his notes. Obviously, many talking course books will say not to do this; yet in this example, we can be pardoning. Knowing the personality of Steve Jobs, he might have deliberately and mindfully chose, intentionally, to utilize notes. As you endeavor to further develop your relational abilities, attempt to not utilize any notes.
 Let's separate the construction of his

 discourse. Opening
 _Body
 Thanks crowd Small joke

Immediately sets up the structure
 Three stories from my life, that's it no big deal, just three stories
 The main story is about:

.Connecting the
 dots Tells story

Starts with end of story - I dropped out of college Asks why did I drop out?
Tells background, tells story
Parents
How he got to college
Story of going to Reed college
Following intuition worked out

.Example: calligraphy
 .Draws back into the point of connecting dots
 Concludes why it's important to connect the dots
 The subsequent story is about .Love and loss .Tells story

Sets up situation
 Presents problem: got fired

.

Asks question of how did this happen?

Something dawned on me

.

Still loved what I did

.

Ties back into what the story is about

Didn't see it then
 None ofthis would have happened if didn't get fired

Got to find what you love
 Drives point about loving what you do How

.

you should keep looking Stops

.

talking about story and tells

.The third story is about .Death

why this is significant Keep looking don't settle
Conclusion

Quote in regards to death

Death and his personal experience and thoughts Tells story about his cancer experience
What it meant to "get your affairs in order" Story is very linear
 Progresses from point to point Situation,
 problem, conclusion

Uses story to build rapport about experience on death "New is you" Directly
communicates to audience Gives advice to audience
 Gets into the students' mindset

 Don't let others tell you what to do

.

Talks about his youth experience

.

Story about a publication he read

·

"When I was your age"

Relates directly to audience

·

Ties the points back together

·

Takes time to set up the significance of the publication

·

"Stay hungry, stay foolish"

Always wished that for myself
And now, as you graduate, I wish that for you .Stay hungry, stay foolish
Does this look recognizable? As may be obvious, his system is very much like the one we talked about in the Golden Personal Pitch.
His diagram follows the equivalent concept:

1. Tell them what you will tell them.
2. Tell them.
3. Tell them what you told them.

The design, the substance, and the conveyance of his discourse were exceptionally straightforward. Since it was so basic, it was not difficult to follow and made it staggeringly successful. Steve Jobs comprehended his crowd, conveyed straightforwardly to them, and successfully made himself clear. The general purpose of correspondence is for your audience to comprehend you clearly.

How To Practice:
Practice by watching extraordinary speakers. This ought to be a wonderful exercise. Extraordinary speakers can rouse, teach, and engage you all simultaneously. Search online for video clasps of individuals that you regard and watch their correspondence. Pick individuals who you accept are extraordinary speakers that you need to imitate. Who are a portion of those individuals for you?
Some models my understudies have referenced include: TED Talks, Steve Jobs, Bill Clinton, Barack Obama, Sheryl Sandberg, Toastmaster addresses, and most loved podcasts.

Extra Challenge:

Watch the video of a speaker that you regard and recount their discourse. Imagine that you are an entertainer and you will convey this present individual's discourse. Track and present the discourse as the speaker moves along.
Practice articulating and saying the words as he says them, gain proficiency with his idiosyncrasies, the hand motions, the stops, and notice every one of the particularities in his discourse. This activity provides you with a sample of the distinctive style that each speaker has. As you progress through your excursion, you will find specific styles that you need to take on and cause your own and different styles that you to don't exactly like.

If you are driving in the vehicle, turn on the live radio or play a discourse that you appreciate. Then repeat his speech along with the speaker. Very much like how you would chime in with a melody you appreciate; talk alongside a talk.

How To Apply:
 As you become more mindful of how others talk, you come out better as a speaker yourself. You can sit in gatherings and recognize what makes your partner's discourse exceptionally hers. Then you can think about yourself. What are the talking characteristics and qualities that you have? If somebody somehow managed to imitate you, how might they sound? What qualities of discourse could they utilize? For instance, it is not difficult to mimic Arnold Schwarzenegger due to his manner of speaking and emphasize. Those are discourse characteristics that are interestingly his. A lesser-realized truth is that he has spent innumerable hours preparing his discourse through training and private mentoring. He is extremely mindful of his articulation and deliberately talks with the emphasize in light of the fact that that is the thing that makes him critical and his film lines quotable. What is it about the manner in which you talk that makes it exceptionally yours?

7. Preparation
"Practice doesn't make great. Just wonderful practice makes perfect."
– Vince Lombardi, NFL Hall of Fame Coach

Proper readiness forestalls horrible showing. How about we return to your first discourse. Place yourself back on that stage, any place it might have been, and ask yourself: who was my crowd? Might it be said that you were conversing with new partners, would you say you were at a new employee screening, or would you say you were giving a show to your supervisors? Recollect that correspondence is tied in with conveying your musings and thoughts to another person. Being familiar with that another person will fundamentally decide how you convey. For instance, would you converse with your 4-year-old kid the same way you would converse with the President of the United States?

Understanding other situational information, such as your environment, will also influence the way you communicate. Talking in a gathering room versus an uproarious café versus a huge amphitheater with an amplifier will change the manner in which you talk. Extraordinary moderators will set aside effort to get their work done and prepare.

  Example arrangement inquiries to pose include:

.

Who will be in the audience when I give this

- presentation? What are the goals of my presentation?

- What impression do I want to leave on my

- audience? How long do I have to present?

- What is the environment

- like? Who else is talking?

- Will this be interactive?

-

What is my takeaway message?

Let's response these inquiries from my understudy Russell's viewpoint. He is a major information engineer at a huge innovation organization and will be giving a show to individuals inside the organization. We should investigate how he can approach the presentation.

Question: What is the organization of the show (this incorporates, time, area, setting, etc.)?

Time: this show will happen in a one-hour meeting. Area:

organization meeting room with a huge oval table. Number of members: around 10-15 organization employees.

Setting: representing the PowerPoint show, then, at that point, sitting for the item demo.

Question: What impression would I like to leave on my crowd? At the point when I am as of now not in the room, what do I need my crowd to think?

After the gathering is finished, I need everybody in the crowd to leave thinking: "Russell is this present organization's master in enormous information innovation. Next time I ponder huge information or have inquiries concerning that subject, I will contemplate Russell."

Question: what are the substance objectives of my presentation? After the show is finished, I need to have instructed my audience: 1) What sort of information is accessible to our company 2) How they can utilize the information tables themselves 3) Best practices on utilizing the data

Question: Who will be in the crowd when I give this presentation? All crowd individuals will be work associates. I have interfaced with 60% of the crowd individuals and the rest will meet me for the first time. Some of the crowd will have specialized designing information, while others have less designing information and more business knowledge.

Question: Do I need this to be interactive?

Yes. Since this is additionally an item demo, I need the crowd to associate with me all through the presentation.

Question: Who else is talking? I will be the essential speaker. Different partners will be available at the meeting,

so they may toll in to address a couple questions.

Question: Why am I giving this presentation?

I've been getting a great deal of messages and inquiries from associates on the best way to utilize the information that the organization is producing. Many individuals are confounded, so I need to tell everybody the best way to utilize it properly.

How To Practice:
Brainstorm and work out a few inquiries to pose to yourself as you get ready for a discourse. You can utilize the inquiries previously recorded and develop them. Then, answer each question with details so that you have a rich visualization of your presentation. Responding to these inquiries, it provides us with an unmistakable feeling of how to structure our show. For instance, we realize that there will be crowd individuals who are meeting me interestingly, so it's important to have a more careful presentation. These inquiries permit us to more readily design our entire discourse, just as art the prologue to be appealing and engaging.

If you are asking yourself, "Is it important to ponder these subtleties?" The response is yes. The more you can imagine your show, the better you can plan and the more sure you will turn into. It resembles playing sports. The better you practice, the better you perform during game time.

The objective isn't flawlessness. The objective is to rehearse with exclusive expectations so when you perform, you will perform at an undeniable level. In the event that you will go through 30 minutes rehearsing your show, milk those 30 minutes for as much squeeze as possible. Put in the greatest energy inside those 30 minutes, and afterward continue on. Assuming you will accomplish something, do it right.

8. Focus on the Introduction

Giving introductions is a period for you to sparkle. Assuming you do this admirably, you can show your worth and intrigue your partners. Be that as it may, assuming you don't catch the crowd's consideration inside the principal minute, you will have lost them for the remainder of great importance. The presentation of your show is basic in being a compelling communicator.

Let's proceed from the situation of Russell from the past part. Since Russell addressed the planning questions, he has greater clearness on the most proficient method to sort out his discussion. Presently, the more itemized design of his presentation looks like this:

Opening

.

Introduction, talk about:

.

My background at the company

.

The team

.

The project

.Engage the audience:

.

Ask the audience, "Can you tell me some of the problems/questions you have about using our data?"

.

Transition: I've also been receiving a lot of emails/questions on this, so that is why my team and I have decided to give this presentation.

.

Agenda

.

For the show, we will discuss:
 One: what kind of data is available to the company? Two: how you can use the data table yourself? Three: best practices on using the data

Then I'll show you a live demo
 And, wrap up with additional top to bottom Q&A

.

"As I' m going through the presentation, feel free to ask me any questions."
Body

.State the main point of your presentation...

Building compatibility is quite possibly the most crucial thing to do while conveying. Simply consider it according to the next individual's perspective. Assuming you met an individual who let you kPresently that he is a web designer who studied software engineering, fabricates versatile applications for the sake of entertainment – and afterward begins conversing with you regarding how to compose PC programming code – you would probably assume the best about him that he knows what he's saying. Now, contrast this and an individual who doesn't enlighten you anything concerning his experience, and promptly begins conversing with you about composing PC code. You may wind up inquiring, "Stand by, who are you? For what reason are you discussing this?"

In a similar manner, your presentation is the place where you assemble affinity with your crowd. This is the place where you assemble legitimate validity. To this end individuals gave close consideration when Steve Jobs talked, or when the President talks; such speakers have as of now settled compatibility with their nearby audience.

Understanding how to be a successful speaker isn 't rocket science. As fundamental as it sounds, having sympathy with your crowd and relating to their sentiments will help altogether. Place yourself in one of the seats of your crowd. It's a Wednesday at 2 p.m. what's more you are sitting in a meeting room at work, planning to pay attention to a show. What is going through you mind? How can you feel at that point? As the moderator, you ought to know that everybody in the crowd is very much like you when you are the one tuning in. When you can comprehend your crowd, you can draw in them. For instance, get going your show with something cheerful; make a wisecrack or a suitably engaging anecdote about the organization all of you work for.

Making the crowd chuckle is a strong method for drawing in the room and to additional form compatibility. Would you rather pay attention to somebody dull, or somebody who attempted to engage you? It's okay to be laugh uncontrollably entertaining. The key idea is commitment. You can draw in the crowd in various ways: ask them inquiries, have them add to the discussion, talk about them straightforwardly so they can without much of a stretch identify with the point you are going to address. Likewise, recollect to smile!

Stating your plan is a compelling method for ensuring your crowd tracks. Measure your plan. All things considered say the numbers"one, two, three." For example,

" First, I'm demonstrating what sort of information is accessible. Second, I will disclose how to utilize the information tables. Third, I will give you best practices on utilizing the data."

It's simple for the human brain to track, since now you are giving them a mathematical guide they can likewise imagine as you speak.

Try not to make any presumptions about the crowd. In the event that you need them to ask you inquiries, then, at that point, unequivocally say you need them to ask you inquiries as you present; don't anticipate that they should do as such freely.

How To Practice:
 This is an extension of what we realized in the Golden Personal Pitch section about
building a compelling opening. Take the readiness questions you finished from the past
part to make a connecting with opening. Find similitudes that individuals have in the
room and recount a carefree tale or tale about it. Use numbers to direct the crowd
through your plan of what you will introduce. Ponder minutes in your show where you
can persistently connect with the crowd part, like halting at a specific region and
inquiring "any inquiries?" prior to continuing on. Use list items to structure your
presentation. Oppose working out the discourse word for word.

Extra Challenge:
 Watch recordings from talks that you appreciate yet just for the principal minute.
Following 60 seconds pass (or even 30 seconds) pause and contemplate what the speaker
did to catch your consideration. Did she pose you an inciting inquiry, did she show you a
convincing visual, or recount to you about an engaging story? Initial feelings can
represent the moment of truth a show. Watch and concentrate how incredible speakers
spend the initial 30 to 60 seconds of their discourse. You might decide to join their
strategies into your own speaking.

9. How to be More Articulate

" It as a rule requires over three weeks to set up an incredible extemporaneous speech."
– Mark Twain

For a considerable lot of my understudies, perhaps their greatest shortcoming and
wanted region to work on in will be in their verbalization, further developing coherency.
Since here most understudies make the greatest enhancements, kindly follow intently
alongside how to practice.

Articulation is made conveyance and 2) content. contemplations in an articulate way that
is reasonable and simple to follow. We should get going with delivery.
 out of basically two perspectives: 1)

 It's tied in with introducing your
 1) Delivery is regarding how you say something.

A lucid individual is brief and clear in their conveyance, similar to a quiet waterway that moves through the forest. The correspondence is at a controlled, certain speed. It is neither too quick nor excessively sluggish. A lucid individual connects with his entire being into imparting, from the verbal correspondence to the non-verbal correspondence. To the audience, the expressive speaker is quiet when talking. The eloquent individual will grin or make any looks that are fitting for the discussion. This is the thing that we call presence.

An understandable person:

.

Does not stutter

.

Does not use um's, uh's, or other filler words

.

Does not use repetitive words such as "like"

.

Does not shift his attention

.

Does not fidget

.

Controls her body language – her arms, feet

.Is fully present in the moment and is very deliberate in what he or she is communicating

Has strong, direct eye focus
 Approach each discussion you have with a companion, associate, and relative as an opportunity to work on being well-spoken. Before you get the telephone or take part in discussion, attempt to be clear with regards to what you are attempting to say. If you don't have anything to say, then don't say anything. This will keep you from rambling.

Here's a model: You are working and you advance toward the espresso machine. Before you show up, you ought to be cognizant that there might be associates there and set yourself up to talk. Take a full breath, not on the grounds that you are anxious, but since you are quiet. The purpose in being quiet is to forestall stammering or talking excessively quick. Unwind and ponder what you are saying.

 2) Content is regarding what is really said.

An expressive individual is organized and coordinated in the thing he is imparting. One normal issue that I see with my understudies is that they will more often than not talk and don't have the foggiest idea where they will wind up. Later all that has been said, it resembles there are a lot of specks on the guide that don't connect.
 By consolidating structure into correspondence, you permit yourself and the audience to come to an obvious conclusion. Far and away superior, the construction sets up building blocks for you to talk about, including more substance top of another idea.

A simple way for you to rehearse your association in ordinary talking is by providing request to what you are going to say. For instance, start your discussions this method for improving your structure:

.

"I have 2 thoughts on that" – and then you might say, "My first thought is..." Then you talk about your first point. You continue by saying, "My second thought is..." Then you talk about your second point.

."The agenda for today's meeting is 1, 2, 3" – then follow the numbers with the categories you want to talk about.

By getting sorted out your musings into a numbered system, you are building up a construction for your audience that is more straightforward to follow than assuming you started looking at everything. Keep in mind, the audience is human, very much like you.

Communication is exceptionally close to home. It's tied in with putting yourself out there and
trading data with another person. The best communicators are ones who are real and are alright with themselves. You never need to be another person; however, obviously, you can concentrate on what makes somebody incredible at talking and gain from those components what to fuse into your own style. Being lucid will take practice. The incredible thing is, each second is a chance to rehearse your enunciation. It's not just when you are giving a huge show, it's the ordinary associations you have with people.

It's totally adequate and trivial assuming you have said anything abnormal to somebody. Use it as a learning opportunity; you can consider that "misstep" and contemplate what you would do another way sometime later. Like some other ability, being lucid will take experimentation, nonstop practice, and realizing what works for you.

As a pre-practice work out, contemplate somebody who you believe is eloquent. This can be a genuine or imaginary individual: the President, your companion, or even a film character like James Bond. Presently ponder why you accept that individual is eloquent. Perhaps this is a result of the volume of their discourse, the way that they don't falter, their manner of speaking, or how their words appear to turn out in a consistent stream. Ask yourself, "What makes that person so well spoken?" If you are able to answer that question, then try to imitate his talk like we did in a previous practice. At last, you will ingest what is valuable and make the verbalization your own.

How To Practice:
The most ideal way to work on further developing your enunciation is to video yourself. In the event that you practice this progression reliably, you will see incredible outcomes in your endeavors. You can do this effectively with your cell phone or PC. Contingent upon your gadget, search online for the most ideal way to record yourself.

If you have a MacBook:
> Open QuickTime Player
> Select "Document" then, at that point "New Movie Recording" > Start recording

It 's ideal to set up the recording the same way you would be giving your discourse. For instance, assuming you will be remaining before a crowd of people, observe a room where the camera can catch your whole body, including your
hands and feel if conceivable. Notwithstanding your looks, you likewise need to notice the remainder of your body language.

Start rehearsing your discourse in lumps. Practice and record the presentation of your discourse, which may be one short lived. Then stop and play it back. Truly study yourself. Then practice the introduction again, this time making adjustments, fixing any mistakes you might have, and making improvements to your communication. Then stop and play it back; honestly critique yourself and continue the process until you feel confident and comfortable with the introduction. Presently you can move on.

Next, separate different pieces of your show as you practice. Pick little pieces that will make it simple for you to practice consistently. At last, you will need to rehearse the entire show, standing up, recording yourself, with no stops.

Here 's a superior visual. At the point when I need to rehearse for an impending discourse, I either observe a vacant gathering room that has no windows or delay until later work hours to utilize the meeting room. It's actually your own inclination as to having a group of people or not— regardless of whether you care that individuals might be watching you practice your show. I will generally appreciate more protection when I'm rehearsing and save the exposure for my genuine presentation.

Practicing on your own implies that you must know about how to improve your show. Apply every one of the parts in this book when you are self-investigating and you ought to have a decent comprehension of what you are doing.

Another method of rehearsing is having your companion Or then again partner watch you. For the most part, you need somebody who has decision making ability on successful correspondence, however you needn't bother with a correspondence master. The point here is that you become more open to standing and freely talking before the individual; and, you can rehearse over and over the thing you are saying. A decent practice accomplice will give you input on explicit regions — for instance, saying"um… uh" too often, stammering, and superfluously rehashing words. Or, the input may bring up that you're saying too much"you know" or you're basically not seeming to be OK in certain places.

Explore the training strategies that turn out best for you. Regardless of how you practice, you should do rehearse. You can't anticipate improving without training. To further develop your coherency, rehearsing by recording yourself on video will give you the best capacity to develop. It might appear to be new and somewhat awkward to watch yourself on record, however sit through it and the video will wake you up to making extraordinary improvements.

You can likewise voice record yourself. In the event that you have time on your drive, take out your telephone and record yourself discussing any subject. Then, at that point, play it back and study yourself.

In synopsis, this counsel is very clear. Set up your PC, telephone, or any gadget that has video recording, and record yourself giving your show. The focus point here is to watch and evaluate yourself on how you can improve.

Extra Challenge
 If you are giving a show with visuals, practice and record yourself in the meeting room. Have your slides shown as you would in the genuine show and go through it like a dress practice. The most awesome method for rehearsing would be if you would rehearse the show multiple times in the genuine setting with the specific crowd that will be in participation during the genuine show. Since that is absurd, you need to mirror the genuine climate however much as could be expected. You can have companions and partners sit in the crowd and give you criticism as well.

10. Non-Verbal Communication on Stage

Even however the setting might transform, one thing will remain something similar – your non-verbal communication. You may have heard individuals say that 80% of correspondence is non-verbal. The genuine rate is begging to be proven wrong, however the idea is valid. Quite a bit of your correspondence is passed on non-verbally.

Non-verbal correspondence is absolutely everything outside of the substance of what you really say. There is an enormous piece of correspondence you might not have seen with regards to non-verbal talking. Non-verbal correspondence is chiefly 1) your non-verbal communication and 2) your actions.

Your non-verbal communication incorporates:

.

Eyes

.

Mouth

.

Arms

.

Legs

Non-verbal communication is entrancing. There are many books that attention only regarding the matter, yet here we will zero in on non-verbal communication as it identifies with you and public talking. We should get going with when you are standing and communicating.

You may feel as you don't have the foggiest idea how to manage your hands. Assuming you need instances of hand motions, watch official addresses. Notice that when the President comes to a meaningful conclusion, he will in general point with his thumb on top of his forefinger. This conveys self-assuredness and decreases the forceful tone of straightforwardly pointing with your pointer. There are numerous blends of hand motions and developments. The key is to observe what you are OK with. Regardless of whether you impersonate the best speaker on the planet, you might look and feel off-kilter, which is definitely not an extraordinary approach to communicate.

To sort out what works for you, work on recording yourself! Allude to the past section and proceed with the activity. At the point when you first practice your discourse, convey it without thinking excessively, as normally as could be expected. Then evaluate yourself.

Ask yourself questions such as:

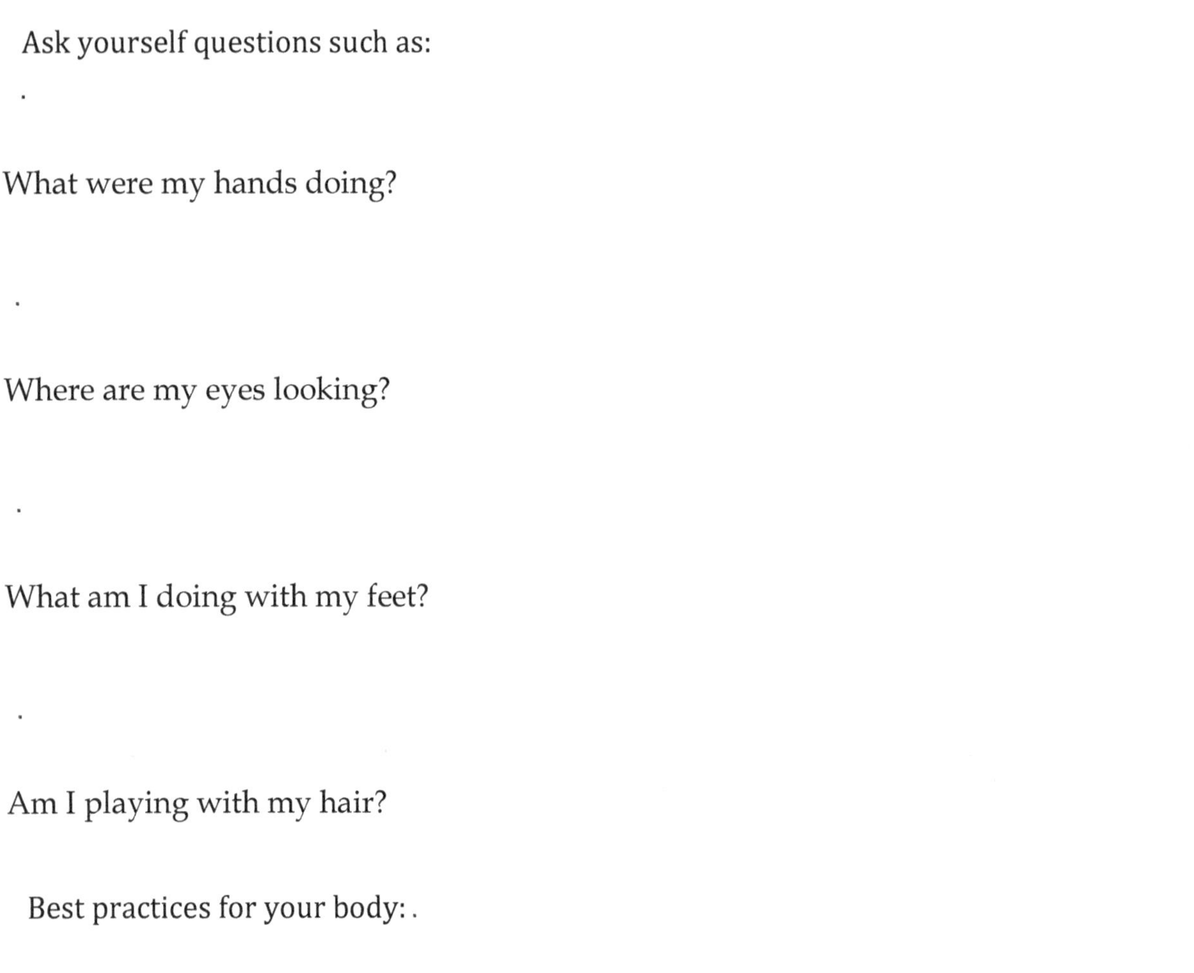

- What were my hands doing?

- Where are my eyes looking?

- What am I doing with my feet?

- Am I playing with my hair?

Best practices for your body: .

If you are unsure what to do with your hands, have them by your side, not in your pockets.

.

As a general rule for your eyes, try to have one focal point you direct your eyes to for each point you are making. After you complete a single point, thought, or sentence, move your gaze to your next focal point.

.

The focal point can be your audience, but it does not have to be. If making eye contact with your listeners makes you nervous, pick a focal point that is in their general direction — such as the wall behind them.

.

When standing, avoid crossing or placing your feet on top of another.

.

Watch your hands as nervousness tends to make people play with their hair, touch their face, or put hands in their pockets.

.

Do not have closed body language such as crossing your arms because that makes you appear closed off to your listeners.

Good non-verbal correspondence will be chiefly your non-verbal communication. The objective is to be sure. Being agreeable and confident, in regards to what you will convey, is the manner by which you acquire certainty. Thus, how would you become more comfortable?

It is vital to address the basic method of being agreeable, as a person. I can advise you to stand and introduce yourself with a particular goal in mind, yet in the event that you are not being your legitimate self, you will look and feel off-kilter in front of an audience. Being agreeable and certain beginnings with your outlook. For instance, assuming you don't have faith in yourself, no other person will. The key is to work on extending trust in the thing you are saying, and others will consider you to be certain when you speak.

Non-verbal correspondence additionally incorporates the garments you wear. Picture this: assuming you see somebody on the news wearing sweats and a t-shirt discussing the law, contrasted with somebody wearing formal attire discussing the law, who might you give greater believability to? Who might you accept to be the legal counselor? Our non-verbal signals all impart something to the world.

Different spaces of non-verbal correspondence are your activities. For example, if you show up late to your presentation, what do you think that conveys to your audience? If you are sitting in the conference room texting away on your mobile phone, then that is also speaking a message. The same way you can comprehend somebody dependent on their activities is the same way somebody can get you, in light of yours. Recall that correspondence is a declaration of yourself, so anything that you do– verbally, non-verbally, through your activities – is imparting some sort of message to your audience.

Mindset Some of my understudies talk at a high speed and may find themselves stammering. Part of the explanation for this is that they are not positive about correspondence. They feel that what they are saying isn't significant, so they need to say it as quick as conceivable in light of the fact that they figure individuals will quit focusing on them. This is valid provided that you make it true.

Instead, you should move your outlook. If you are giving a tenminute presentation to your colleagues, then bask in the glory of those ten minutes. You realize that regardless, you have ten minutes in front of an audience that nobody can detract from you. As it were, they are "constrained" to pay attention to you. You don't need to be anxious about the possibility that that they will leave or become diverted. You have the stage and no other person. The way that you are giving a show implies that your associates as of now accept you have something vital to say; if not, you would not be offered the chance to give the show. This implies that for those ten minutes, you have the chance to be the master regarding the matter you are talking about. Assuming you have ranking directors in the gathering, don't imagine that they know more than you.

Rather, with regards to the subject you are talking about, you know more than they. For what other reason would they say they are setting aside the effort to pay attention to you? You have something important to say and your partners need to hear what you need to say, so take as much time as necessary. Unwind, feel good, and tell them precisely what you need to tell them.

Overcoming self-uncertainty and anxiety helped a companion of mine become a more loosened up open speaker. We'll call her Judy. Judy discovered that needing the endorsement of others a lot of is an enormous barricade in communicating certainty in front of an audience. "I had joined my nearby Toastmasters' Club, yet my apprehension would not disappear," chuckles Judy. "It appeared to be that consistently, I was gaining zero headway. But finally, the president of the club called me aside. He said, 'Judy, your concern is that you're needing us to like you. Move past that! At the point when you get up to talk, tell us — as far as you could tell, that is — to plunk down, be calm and tune in. Lead us to where you need us to go! Get up there and act sure, assume responsibility for the room, and acknowledge we want to hear what you need to say.'" Judy says she accepted his recommendation. The following time she got up to talk, she took order of the room, dumped the requirement for endorsement, and aced the show. Judy never felt all that apprehensive again, and she's spoken in many circumstances from that point forward. (This last passage was really composed by Judy herself!)

How To Practice
 This is an expansion of the video practice with an attention on your nonverbal
communication. Record yourself so you can see your whole body, from head to toe if
conceivable. Be intensely perceptive on how you manage your body: your hands, fingers,
arms, eyes, mouth, feet, everything. Stop every now and then to get a freeze outline, to
find in a solitary second the thing you are doing and what you are talking with your non-
verbal communication. The objective of this, obviously, is to improve. Record yourself,
speak, notice, and afterward record yourself once more — this time making the right
improvements.

Extra Challenge
 Breathing activities may likewise help. Work on taking some profound breathes in and
breathes out when you feel snapshots of nervousness. A portion of my understudies have
chosen to commit 5 minutes consistently to sitting peacefully to rehearse profound
relaxing. This aides clear their brains and gives them more command over their nerves.
Once in a while, my understudies may likewise choose to stay there peacefully to think —
with the goal that when they talk, they try not to meander aimlessly and talking at a high
speed. You may likewise choose to fuse reflection into your training. Have a good time
and test with techniques that will assist you with controlling and quiet your psyche in
manners that are best for you.

11. Who is Your Audience, Really?

Communication will forever, consistently, affect someone else or thing. By definition,
correspondence is about the trading of data starting with one point then onto the next.
Along these lines, it is crucial to foster a profound comprehension of your crowd. At the
point when you are getting ready, ask yourself, "Who is my audience?"

 Some instances of who your crowd may be:

 .

Colleagues

 .

Friends

Family

Investors

College students

Managers

Fitness enthusiasts

Potential clients

Marketers
 You need to comprehend your crowd however much as could reasonably be expected. Similarly we speak with our kids uniquely in contrast to the manner in which we speak with our supervisors, we should perceive that who our crowd is will shape the manner in which we impart. The more nitty gritty depictions of a crowd of people you can give, the better.

Here's an illustration of how Russell dove further into understanding his audience.

Audience:

Colleagues

How many? 10-15.

.Do we know each other? I know 50% of the people in attendance.

What departments are they in? Half are from the software department, the other half are from the advertising team.

What do we all have in common? Everyone in the room is married with children.

What is everyone's age? I think they are all 30 -45 years of age.

What is the gender breakdown? Mostly males, 25% females.

Do they have expertise in the content I am presenting? I will be talking about the technical aspects of how to use data tables. I don't think any of them understands it to the level that I do. I have to explain concepts simply, so they have a clear understanding of what I'm talking about.

This permits you to picture the crowd you will talk. It likewise provides you with a superior feeling of who you are imparting to, which influences how you convey. In this model, you can conceptualize that you may get going catching everybody's eye in the space of normal interests. You can discuss wedded existence with kids so everybody can identify with one another. As you get into the show, you will need to clarify ideas in straightforward terms, on the grounds that from your crowd investigation, you realize that not every person has inside and out specialized knowledge.
 This is a comparative way to deal with a business understanding its customers.

When an organization initially begins, they need to comprehend their specialty market. They pose comparable inquiries to recognize their crowd, their clients. What is my client segment? Who am I offering to? What are they keen on? Where do they hang out? How would I get my message to them?

Basically, a business distinguishing a commercial center and you recognizing your crowd is all correspondence. Correspondence is at the principal underlying foundations of what we do in the public eye. Regardless of whether you work in huge groups, little groups, no groups, you are imparting to the world. Even as you are reading this book right now, we are engaging in communication. In the first place, I am trading my data with you by offering you my thoughts. Then, the way that you have bought this book has provided some data back to me. Once more, make it a highlight know your crowd since that is the establishment of communication.
 How To Practice:
 Think pretty much every one individuals you will interact with today, or this week, and show them out. You can begin by gathering them, then, at that point, going further into understanding.

 This week you may meet with one companion or a gathering of companions. Ask:
 .

How many?

What age?

How we do we know each other?

What do we have in common?

What do we find humorous?

Why are we friends?

What do we know about each other?

And the list can continue…

Use this activity to work on distinguishing your crowd. When you practice this more, you'll start to see that you will normally pose yourself these inquiries as you participate in discussion with somebody. This can make you a superior conversationalist, since now you have many subjects (identified with spaces of interest, as in the rundown of inquiries above) to discuss. This is an incredible method for rehearsing, in light of the fact that you will presumably interface with individuals significantly more frequently than you will give introductions. When you get to your show readiness, you can distinguish your crowd with more accuracy to assist you with feeling more good and sure. The additional advantage of this activity is that by showing interest in the other individual, the person will be more keen on you, and you will have better conversations!

Extra Challenge:

When you see an advertisement, ask yourself, "Who is the audience that this company is communicating to?" Define the audience by asking yourself questions such as the ones listed here and then expand on those questions to get a deeper understanding. Practice this with any commercial you may experience consistently. It very well may be a business, a print show by the bus station, a web-based notice, or a radio message. Whatever the promotion, the organization is very much aware of the message they are conveying and that organization has done a comparable exercise in characterizing its audience.

12. Putting the Pieces Together
"Life resembles riding a bike. To keep your surplus, you should keep moving."
- Albert Einstein

Here is the place where we set up the discourse! Now you ought to have a great deal of your materials all set. How about we go through the means on the most proficient method to make your presentation.

Review: Your objectives, shortcomings, and qualities. Allude back to lessons: .

2. What are your goals?

.

3. Be Honest About Your Weaknesses

.

4. Build on Your Strengths

You don 't need to do anything extra here. The place of this progression is for you to be incredibly perceptive of your objectives, shortcomings, and strengths.

Step 1: Create a blueprint of your show. Allude back to lessons:

.

5. The Golden Personal Pitch

.

6. Dissecting Greatness: Steve Jobs

.7. Preparation
.8. Focus on the Introduction

Remember to utilize list items to keep your show structure brief and compact. In this progression, you don't have to work out or convey the entire discourse presently. You might have effectively finished these activities. Assuming this is the case, use your current material and continue.

Step 2: Develop your speech.

You have a few choices here and your decisions will rely upon your own inclinations. Here you begin conveying your presentation.

Here are a few choices that my understudies tracked down supportive when putting their discourse together.

Option 1: Go through your shot pointed construction and begin working out the words that you need to say.

Recall the model in illustration 8. Zero in on the Introduction.

Here is the first slug structure:
Opening

.

Introduction, talk about:

.

My background at the company

.

The team

.

The project

.

Engage the audience:

.

Ask the audience, "Can you tell me some of the problems/questions you have about using our data?"

Transition: "I've also been receiving a lot of emails/questions on this, so that is why my team and I decided to give this presentation."

Agenda

For the show, we will discuss:
One: What kind of data is available to the company? Two: How you can use the data table yourself? Three: Best practices on using the data.

Then, I'll show you a live demo.
And wrap up with more in-depth Q&A.
.Body
"As I'm going through the show, go ahead and ask me any questions."
Main point to be discussed...

Here is the means by which my understudy worked out the words to his presentation:
Opening
[Introduction] "Good morning, everyone. For those that do not know me, my name is Russell and I am the company's big data architect. For the colleagues that I work with already (insert light- hearted funny comment later)."

[Engage the audience] "Before I begin the presentation, can you guys tell me what are some of the problems or questions you have about using our data?" (Field the answers from the audience). "That's great to hear. I've also been receiving a lot of emails and questions about similar issues, and this is exactly why my team and I decided to put this presentationtogether. I'll be able to address your questions throughout the presentation. We also have time for Q&A towards the end."
[Agenda] "As for the agenda today, we will be discussing three areas."

.

1) What kind of data is available to the company?

.

2) How you can use the data table yourself.

.

3) Best practices on using the data.

.

"Finally, we'll wrap up with a live demo and more in -

depth Q&A. As I'm going through the presentation, feel free to ask me any questions. The person who asks the best question will get freecoffee!"

Then Russell will keep working out different spaces of his discourse. In this technique, Russell is plunking down before his PC while talking and composing the expressions of his show. Recollect that composed correspondence is not the same as spoken show. Try not to compose your discourse like a novel, rather compose how you would conversationally speak.

Option 2: Using your construction, convey and emphasize as you come. Allude back to illustration 9: How to be More Articulate (and how to practice).

Take the construction of your discourse and have it before you, so it 's effectively distinguishable yet not such a lot of that you are perusing off of the page. Set up your video recorder so it can record you, as though you were giving the real
 show. You can decide to either sit or stand, whichever you like as of now. As we talked about in the past example, you will ultimately need to replicate your real climate where you'll talk, however much as could be expected, when you practice

Then utilize the design as a psychological diagram and really convey your show. Say your total sentences as though you were conversing with a genuine crowd before you. The construction resembles having list cards that you use as an aide. You are never perusing off of the aide; to that end we kept them in list item design. This strategy will keep you from needing to remember your discourse in exactly the same words. Remembering your discourse takes additional time, and it runs the danger that assuming you fail to remember a line, it is hard to easily review the remainder of your discourse. This might upset your general stream and conveyance. It is likewise conceivable that you will sound excessively practiced and unnatural. That might occur assuming you retain your discourse since you begin to sound not so much conversational but rather more discourse like. All things considered, in any case, there are times while retaining your discourse is more great. If you were delivering a speech in front of a large audience that is more like a performance, such as a TEDTalk, then memorizing your speech would be ideal. But if you were giving a presentation to your colleagues in the conference room, using a structure as a guide would be the better option so you can sound more conversational.

From here, say your speech aloud; then stop and write down further notes on what you want to say or any edits you want to make. My students will usually speak first, then write it down, speak it again, and then write it down again — this time refining the content. This turns into an iterative cycle as you come all through the show. You can do this in pieces. Start with the introduction, then the first point of the body, then the second point, and so forth. At last you will have created your whole speech.

Option 3: Use the construction and practice a couple of dry runs. This choice will most likely take minimal measure of time, yet is a further developed since there is less readiness and practice included. Like Option 2, accept your design as an aide, stand up, and convey your show. It is ideal to video record, or possibly voice record yourself. Then, play back the recording and make improvements based on your feedback.
  You don't need to record your substance in exactly the same words. You are conveying your discourse as far as possible. The more occasions you go through it, the
 more cognizant you ought to turn into. Video recording will be extremely useful in this process.

This implies that in the genuine show, you will convey it the same way. You could possibly have your aide before you, which is dependent upon you, and whatever other assets that you have. According to an optical show perspective, it is ideal assuming that you don't have any notes as you're introducing. On the off chance that you are extending a PowerPoint for instance, you might have the advantage of setting notes in your slides. Practice a couple of run-throughs utilizing the construction until you feel good and certain with your performance.

Step 3: Add in your style.
Allude back to lessons:

.

8. Focus on the Introduction

.

9. How to be More Articulate

.

10. Non-Verbal Communication on Stage

.

11. Who is Your Audience, Really?

.

13. How to Use Visual Aides

.

14. How to Spice Up Your Presentation

The last two examples are later this current section. You should have a general understanding of how your speech is developing first, then you can insert visual aides and add other enhancements to spice up your presentation. As you are making your show, ponder how you can add a greater amount of your own style and flavor to your talking. Utilize these examples as a method for conceptualizing and make the ideal presentation.

How To Practice:
 Put your discourse together! This can be your Golden Personal Pitch, a show for your organization, or whatever other discourse that you have coming up. Utilize these means to direct you through creating your best discourse. Make sure to use every one of the apparatuses accessible to assist you with improving. This implies on the off chance that you have a video recorder, a voice recorder, or even a companion to watch you, these assistants will assist you with turning into a more successful public speaker and
 communicator.

Extra Challenge: Teach these ideas to a companion or associate! The best trial of understanding a bunch of abilities is on the off chance that you can show the ideas to another person. In the event that you have the chance, be a mentor to somebody who is rehearsing public talking. By assessing others, you will foster more grounded feelings of how to make yourself better.

13. How to Use Visual Aides
"Available to be purchased: Baby shoes, never worn."
- Ernest Hemingway

Visuals associates can powerfully affect a show. Assuming you 've at any point watched a TED talk, you will see the perfect, clear visuals that are utilized. Did you had at least some idea that TED has a devoted group to assisting the moderators with making shocking visuals and give enrapturing introductions? They have fostered a recipe that turns out extraordinary for the TED stage.

There are numerous classes of introductions that you can give: an item demo, specialized introductions, group building introductions, introductions on your enthusiasm, and the rundown continues. Albeit every show has various messages, the standards on the best way to convey a viable show apply to every one of them. You can apply comparable standards to adding visuals to your speeches.

Rule #1: One Point Per Visual.

Each visual you choose to utilize ought to just have one primary message. If you are trying to convey more than one message with one slide, then your message becomes unclear. Correspondence is about a having a consistent, intelligent progression of data. Having more than each message in turn resembles having three individuals attempting to let you know something else all simultaneously. Assuming you have more than one message, sort out which is the significant point you are attempting to make and keep it on that visual. Then, move the other important points to the next visuals. This is an incredible method for separating and diminish how much data you present. You need the message to be concise, having importance and effect. Eliminate the focuses that are weak.

Rule #2: Keep It Simple.

The visual ought to be handily perceived. Regardless of whether you are giving a specialized show, and you are disclosing programming code used to fabricate the product, you need to ponder what is unnecessary data and what is the most applicable data. If you have too much information, then it becomes overly complex. A show that is excessively mind boggling isn't great since you are not immediate with regards to your message. As the moderator, you want
 the crowd to see precisely the thing you are attempting to pass on; in any case, you let completely go. Decrease the messiness and present just what is fundamental.

One example is to have a large, high-quality picture take up most of the space, then include some text over the image. Here's a sample:

Recollect that the visual ought to be a help material. What do you think it is supporting here? The speaker might be discussing the development in land and lodging openings. This visual conveys a message to the crowd that this lodging extension is simply starting. The speaker can utilize this to speak further about the topic.

There are different books and materials that discussion about visual helpers. Assuming you are attempting to fund-raise for your organization and you are giving a financial backer show, there are best practices that you can observe online that diagram how you ought to convey the show, particularly assuming it is in PowerPoint.

Rule #3: Your Presentation Dictates the Visuals (the Visuals don't direct you).

Create a blueprint before you set up slides. One normal slip-up I see among my understudies is that when they are informed they will be giving a show, their initial step is to open PowerPoint and put together a few slides. They wind up putting together their whole show with respect to the slides and are now and again compelled to squeeze focuses into the slides since they are there.

Instead, you ought to make a blueprint of your show first. Allude back to the spaces in this book that discussion about structure. As you put together
 the construction (the list items) of your show, that is the point at which you begin to envision where (and which) visuals would be generally useful. The misstep is that individuals assemble the show around the visuals. You should build the presentation first, know what you are going to say, then have the visuals as a complement to your presentation. In outline, contemplate your slides last.

If you need to see an extraordinary public show that viably utilizes visual helpers, watch a TEDTalk or watch Steve Jobs disclose the iPhone. Notice how their visuals are exceptionally clear, exact, and have one primary message. They likewise seldom check out the actual visuals in light of the fact that the speakers are the ones recounting the story — involving the visuals as enhancements, and maintaining the emphasis on the speaker.

How To Practice:
Use this diagram to assemble your speech:

1. Opening
 a. Captures crowd attention b. Leads into discourse topic

2. Body
 a. Main point

i. Subpoint
ii. Support material
b. Main point
i. Subpoint
ii. Support material
c. Main point
i. Subpoint

ii. Support material
3. Conclusion
a. Review or summary
b. Call to activity or essential statement

Be certain you make your construction first, before you begin thinking about visuals. Later you have planned your show, attempt to develop the focuses, remaining inside the short list item attitude. Later your discourse is delineated, embed the regions where adding a visual will lastingly affect your show. You can consider your visuals the help materials that truly assist the crowd with recollecting your significant focuses. The most regularly utilized visuals are slides in a PowerPoint presentation.

You can also choose other visuals such as a live computer demo, a poster, or a physical object. Stay away from little visuals that are difficult to see. Remember that you need each visual to be distinguishable by the whole crowd and not just the first line. A strong visual will drive your message home.

Extra Challenge

After you wrap up with your shot blueprint, nonchalantly toss some visuals together. They don't need to be carefully ready. This additional test is so that you might see what your visual will really resemble. Commonly, when we structure photos of the visuals we need showed in our mind, it will turn out a piece in an unexpected way. This activity will permit you to repeat on your discourse and visuals at the equivalent time.

14. How to Spice Up Your Presentation

Review your show and ponder the regions that might be more confounded for your crowd to comprehend. In those spaces, use analogies. Assuming I pitched you on another organization that associates pet people with each other, and enables them to associate with one another with regards to their pets, it's a lot more straightforward for me to say: "It resembles a Facebook for animal people." Using analogies is powerful on the grounds that you are expanding on top of an idea individuals as of now understand.

In brain science it's called blueprints. Individuals foster patterns dependent on their background and understandings. For instance, assuming you spot an individual wearing a decent formal attire, your blueprint lets you know that this individual is likely a money manager in light of the fact that your background and your presence of mind point you in that direction.

Compare the new idea you are clarifying with an idea your crowd as of now gets it. For instance, when a modeler fabricates another house for a customer, he will contrast the new house and an old house so the customer can make a smooth progress into understanding the distinctions and upgrades in the new house.

Remember to grin! A strong speaker partakes in the occasion, is loose, agreeable, and sure being before the crowd. Grinning will evoke those characteristics. Nonetheless, don't constrain yourself to grin and phony being agreeable to the place where it's inauthentic. Assuming it's unnatural, it will show in your essence and individuals will see it. Grin and unwind; let it come to you normally. Assuming you don't feel it and you are somewhat apprehensive and restless, that is totally fine. Slowly inhale and attempt to partake in the occasion. Be honest to what your identity is and what you are going to impart to your audience.

Demonstrate your initiative by making suggestions. Making ideas on prescribed procedures gives you administration request since you are making an important framework for your partners in the event that they follow your recommendation. For instance, make the suggestion that before you email your care staff, you might possibly track down a prompt arrangement by going into the organization wiki manual to look for the issue you are encountering. Cause suggestions to your associates that will to be valuable.

If you have significant focuses you need to accentuate, rehash yourself.
For instance, you need to let your partners that know if you need to
eliminate an inquiry that you made in the information base, you must kill
the job
physically. You can offer something like, "you should kill the occupation physically,
alright? Kill the occupation physically." Slow down your discourse so individuals can
track and underscore your point again by
rehashing the message.
You might have heard others say this in their show: "Assuming
there's one thing for you to recall from this show, it's… " You might decide
to utilize this assuming that there is a key action item that you need the
crowd part to leave with. If they do not remember anything else after you are
finished, as long as they remember to "kill the job manually," then you will
have been effective in your presentation.
Conclude your show with strength. Commonly, individuals will
tragically have a feeble completion. They will offer something like, "And uh,
better believe it, that is my show. So… any inquiries?" Then they might
disregard or give a low certainty body motion. Notwithstanding, you need to
begin solid and end solid. In your decision, wrap up by summing up what
was talked about and end it purposely. A strong speaker is one that knows
what they need to say and quits talking when they have finished their
message. For: "all in all, today we examined 1) the various information
sources, 2) accepted procedures on managing information issues, and 3) how
to get to the information. That finishes up my show, and presently we will
open it up for Q&A." Period. There is a sure certainty that is conveyed when
you have an exact consummation, since it lets the crowd know that you know
what you need. You need to end it here. Period.

How To Practice:
Go through your discourse and find regions where you may enliven the show by adding
a portion of these elements:

.

Make analogies and comparisons

.

Smile and connect with your audience

.

Make recommendations to the group

.

Repeat important points

.

Have a key takeaway; let the audience know this is the most important part of the presentation

.

Have a strong, deliberate ending

Extra Challenge:
 Watch a show you partake in the entire way through and don't take any notes; simply watch. Later you are done, pause and ponder what you recollect from the show. Then ask yourself why you remember those points. You may find that you recollected the speaker's primary point concerning why having medical care protection is significant in light of the fact that she outlined it with a relationship to wearing a safety belt while driving. Contemplate what made the speaker powerful in getting you, as the memorable audience, her points.
 How did she keep you drew in and mindful? Odds are she utilized a portion of these strategies to brighten up her presentation.

15. Interview Skills: The STAR Approach

The STAR Approach is an incredible way to deal with addressing inquiries questions. It's a structure for how to ponder and respond to inquiries on your feet.

STAR stands for:

Situation: portray the foundation of the circumstance and present your audience with the problem.
Task: what was your objective, what were you attempting to accomplish or tackle from the situation?

Action: what move did you make to attempt to address the problem? Result: what was the result of the activity and how could it settle the problem?

This is viable in light of the fact that organizations need to recruit individuals who will assist the organization with developing. If you can show that your efforts have made the company better, then you will be a valuable candidate. Utilizing the STAR Approach permits you to outline your encounters in a manner to depict how you took a circumstance and improved it for your group and company.

Two or three tips:

.

Do talk with specifics – use numbers, percentages, and examples when it's appropriate. It's easier for someone to visualize and understand specific examples. This makes what you are describing more engaging.

.

Don't speak in generalities – avoid being vague and nondescriptive. Which do you think communicates a message stronger: "I increased the revenue of our company," or "I increased the revenue of our company by $1 million through reducing our sales team time spent on selling underperforming products."
When my understudies initially begin utilizing this methodology, they will more often than not talk as far as consensuses and things not explicit to them. This is your second to feature yourself and the worth that you offer of real value. Be pretty much as explicit as conceivable so you can introduce a convincing answer.

For instance, say the questioner poses you the inquiry: "Enlighten me concerning a time you made an improvement to the organization." Here is the way my understudy utilized the STAR approach for his answer:

Situation: "When I joined the organization, there was no such thing as a major information stage. In any case, as innovation improved, we began producing a great deal of information that we couldn't use and this turned into a problem."

Task: "My objective was to lead a group to plan and modeler a stage that would make the immense measures of information sources accessible for the organization to use."

Action: "I looked for input from my associates who were working in the area and introduced the thoughts on how the organization should plan the huge information stage to the supervisory crew. I then worked with management to hire the right engineers and built the platform."

Result: "Following a while of building and incorporation, we are presently an information driven organization. 70% of our business choices are made dependent on the information that we produce utilizing the large information stage. For instance, we settled on the choice to fuse Facebook login and settled the most repeating checkout issues, which further developed our change rate by 3%."

This is a compact response. Russell gets going by expressing the unique circumstance, providing the audience with the foundation of the circumstance, and he additionally states why this is significant. Then, he clarifies his arrangements for tackling the issue and the move steps he made to arrive at the objective. At long last, he finishes up with the effect. From his clarification, the questioner gets a superior, more certain impression of Russell. Through the STAR approach, Russell exhibits he steps up in taking care of significant issues and makes a critical effect through cooperation. He likewise introduced his thoughts in an unmistakable and coordinated manner.

An improvement to his reaction is add more insights regarding the circumstance. What's the significance here by"a great deal of information"? He might have been more explicit by saying, "We began creating information from our new client base of 1 million, yet we didn't have a stage to use any of this information." Being more itemized reinforces your point since it makes it simpler for the audience to comprehend and recall. All things considered, Russell gave an incredible response.

How To Practice:

Use the STAR way to deal with answer these meeting arrangement questions: .

When did you fail and what did you learn from it?

.

What is your great achievement?

.Give me an example of what differentiates you from your colleagues?

.

How do you handle working with a difficult teammate?

.

How do you utilize your greatest strength?

.

What was the most difficult period in your life and how did you deal with it?

.

Have you ever improved the process of a task at work?

Extra Challenge:
 Ask yourself much more troublesome inquiries! You can look through on the web or imagine that you are the questioner. What inquiries would you pose a candidate?
 What hard inquiries would you pose to a likely recruit to make him sweat?

16. How to ask Spontaneous Questions

Some of my understudies are excessively reluctant with regards to talking and it makes them reluctant to pose inquiries in a gathering setting.
 During a gathering you may be reluctant to pose inquiries since you don't need the spotlight to turn on you, in the event that you may be posing an awful inquiry. You are uncertain in the event that the inquiry you are posing to will be a decent one or a moronic question.

The base of the issue is being outside of your usual range of familiarity. To take care of this issue, you should put stock in yourself and have the certainty to pose the inquiry. It may end up being an awful inquiry. That is adequate, in light of the fact that you will commit the error and gain from it. In the future, you'll know not to pose those kinds of inquiries. You want to constrain yourself to pose the inquiry, assuming it's something at the forefront of your thoughts, and you will start to foster the certainty to ask it — paying little heed to what others think. This is an outlook sort of arrangement. Do you believe the question you are about to ask is a good question? If you do believe it for yourself, then ask it. You are making a legitimate judgment and that is all that truly matters. If you are asking a question for the sake of trying to impress your colleagues or others in the room, then you have a higher risk of asking an unfashionable question.

By rehearsing a large number of the activities depicted in this book, you should encounter an improvement in your public talking and generally speaking relational abilities. With this increment in certainty, posing unconstrained inquiries ought to continuously become more straightforward to deal with. I truly want to believe that you have been practicing!

You can likewise guess what the reaction may be. Pose yourself the inquiry and figure what sort of reaction you may get. Be insightful with regards to the inquiry you are thinking about to pose. This can give you a superior sense assuming that you ought to pose the inquiry. Posing inquiries is great; it keeps you intrigued and permits you to remain occupied with the discussion. This applies in all instances of discourse, regardless of whether it's one-on-one, during an organization show, or before a huge crowd.

What makes a decent question?
The expected answer goes beyond "yes" or "no"
The question expands on the knowledge of the topic If you believe it is a good question
(assuming you were attentive to the speech)
It leads to further discussion
It is asked coherently

How To Practice
As you read a book or article, watch a show, or interaction any kind of data, begin to
conceptualize and record questions you have. Gather a rundown of inquiries and make
presumptions on what you figure the response would be. Posing great inquiries is an
ability. You can find a great deal about an individual and their commitment in the subject
by the inquiries she pose. The more you train your mind to pose inquiries, the better
inquiries you will ask. Extra Challenge
Take the rundown of inquiries that you have and assess them. Investigate the inquiries
and give objective input to yourself to audit on the off chance that the inquiries you have
were smart. Assuming that a portion of the inquiries are not, change the inquiries and
sort out what language you may adjust to make them great inquiries to ask.

Congratulations!

Showtime!
"All the world's a stage."
– William Shakespeare

You presently have the devices to further develop your talking abilities. For you to make
genuine enhancements, you should rehearse. Practice without anyone else, with a
companion, and go out into the world and practice. Recall that your stage can generally
change yet your abilities will forever remain with you. Practice your public talking and
relational abilities by the water cooler, when you are out somewhere else with your
companions, and love the chances to introduce before an audience.

Go forward and deliver!
I hope everything turns out great for you of karma in arriving at your objectives!

www.ingramcontent.com/pod-product-compliance
Lightning Source LLC
Chambersburg PA
CBHW080501030726
47592CB00011B/3206